Pebble™

Woodland Animals

Opossums

by William John Ripple

Consulting Editor: Gail Saunders-Smith, PhD
Consultant: Daniel K. Rosenberg, Assistant Professor
College of Natural Resources, Utah State University

Capstone
press

Mankato, Minnesota

Pebble Books are published by Capstone Press,
151 Good Counsel Drive, P.O. Box 669, Mankato, Minnesota 56002.
www.capstonepress.com

1 2 3 4 5 6 11 10 09 08 07 06

Library of Congress Cataloging-in-Publication Data
Ripple, William John.
    Opossums / by William John Ripple.
    p. cm.—(Pebble books. Woodland animals)
    Summary: "Simple text and photographs present opossums, how they look,
where they live, and what they do"—Provided by publisher.
    Includes bibliographical references and index.
    ISBN-13: 978-0-7368-4248-8 (hardcover)
    ISBN-10: 0-7368-4248-9 (hardcover)
    1. Opossums—Juvenile literature. I. Title. II. Series: Woodland animals.
QL737.M34R56 2006
599.2'76—dc22   2004027187

The author dedicates this book to his nephew Kail Vaith and niece Lindzie Vaith of
Lesterville, South Dakota.

Note to Parents and Teachers

The Woodland Animals set supports national science standards
related to life science. This book describes and illustrates opossums.
The photographs support early readers in understanding the text. The
repetition of words and phrases helps early readers learn new words.
This book also introduces early readers to subject-specific vocabulary
words, which are defined in the Glossary. Early readers may need
assistance to read some words and to use the Table of Contents,
Glossary, Read More, Internet Sites, and Index sections of the book.

Table of Contents

What Are Opossums?

Opossums are mammals with long, thin tails and pointed noses.

Opossums have white, gray, and brown fur.

areas where opossums live

Where Opossums Live

Opossums live in forests
and grasslands.
They live in North America,
Central America,
and South America.

Body Parts

Opossums have many sharp teeth. They also have long claws.

Female opossums
have pouches.
A young opossum
rides around
in its mother's pouch.

Opossums have long tails.
Young opossums
use their tails
to help them climb trees.

What Opossums Do

Opossums play dead
to stay safe
from predators.
Foxes and hawks
hunt opossums.

Opossums look
for food at night.
They eat bugs, berries,
and small animals.

Opossums make dens.
They rest in dens
during the day.

Glossary

forest—land covered mostly by trees; forests are also called woodlands.

grassland—a large area of mostly flat land covered by grass and other small plants

mammal—a warm-blooded animal with hair or fur; female mammals feed milk to their young.

pouch—a pocket on the belly of a female opossum; young opossums live in the pouch for three months after they are born.

predator—an animal that hunts other animals for food

teeth—hard, white bones in the mouth used for biting and chewing; opossums have more teeth than any other North American mammal.

Read More

Jacobs, Lee. *Opossum.* Wild America. San Diego: Blackbirch Press, 2003.

Macken, JoAnn Early. *Opossums.* Animals that Live in the Forest. Milwaukee, Wis.: Weekly Reader Early Learning, 2005.

Whitehouse, Patricia. *Opossums.* What's Awake. Chicago: Heinemann, 2003.

Internet Sites

FactHound offers a safe, fun way to find Internet sites related to this book. All of the sites on FactHound have been researched by our staff.

Here's how:

1. Visit *www.facthound.com*
2. Type in this special code **0736842489** for age-appropriate sites. Or enter a search word related to this book for a more general search.
3. Click on the **Fetch It** button.

FactHound will fetch the best sites for you!

Index

Word Count: 106
Grade: 1
Early-Intervention Level: 11

Editorial Credits

Martha E. H. Rustad, editor; Patrick D. Dentinger, set designer; Ted Williams, book
designer; Wanda Winch, photo researcher; Scott Thoms, photo editor

Photo Credits

Bruce Coleman Inc./Alan Blank, 12; Gary Meszaros, cover; Leonard Lee Rue III, 4
Corbis/Lynda Richardson, 20
Corel, 8
David Liebman, 1; David Liebman/Roger Raegot, 18
Erwin and Peggy Bauer, 14
Minden Pictures/Konrad Wothe, 10
Tom & Pat Leeson, 6
Visuals Unlimited/Steve Maslowski, 16